ALL'S WELL THAT ENDS

PAUL BIRTILL

Paul Birtill was born in Walton, Liverpool in 1960, but now lives in London. He has published a number of collections with Hearing Eye, including *New and Selected poems*. He has also had several of his plays staged at London theatres, including *Squalor* which was shortlisted for the Verity Bargate Award.

ALL'S WELL THAT ENDS
Paul Birtill

ISBN 978-1903110911

First published in this edition 2022 by Wrecking Ball Press.

Cover design: humandesign.co.uk

Supported using public funding by
ARTS COUNCIL ENGLAND
LOTTERY FUNDED

ACKNOWLEDGEMENTS:

Some of these poems first appeared in Poetry Review,
Morning Star and Ambit.

CONTENT

MORE OF THE SAME

I've ate
I've drank
I've laughed
I've dreamt
I've read
I've written
I've walked
I've run
I've listened
I've seen
I've fought
and made up
I've travelled
got drunk
been happy and sad
I've been thin
I've been fat
I've been angry
and unkind
I've learnt
I've succeeded
I've failed
and gone mad
I've been good
I've been indifferent
I've been selfish and bad
I've been ill
I've been well
I'm nearly sixty
What the hell!

NEXT PANDEMIC

I've just been reading about
an old lady of 108 who died
of Coronavirus. Her daughter
said that she had remembered
the Spanish flu epidemic of 1918
which killed fifty million worldwide.
Her doctor at the time told her she had
nothing to worry about and would live
another hundred years.

DANCING

I once asked my father if he danced much
as a young man. 'No I became a Catholic'
he said. It's true most English Catholics
don't go in for all that erotic body movement.
The jive and the jitterbug were not for them,
and they don't like to be seen naked either.
Catholics just can't loosen up – they wear
overcoats in summer and thick pyjamas in bed,
even on their wedding night.

FOUR TIMES

I recall once drinking in a bar
with a schoolmate, both of us underage
and we got talking to an old man who told us
he'd had sexual intercourse four times in his life.
'Four times!' my mate exclaimed laughing loudly –
'that's not much.' 'It's all I wanted' said the old man.
Four times though seemed quite a lot to me then, having
had no sexual experience.

KINDRED SPIRIT

I was telling the priest in confession
how fed up I was with life. 'I'm not surprised'
he said, 'it's a load of boring dog-dirt.
I don't know what God was thinking of when
he created so much rubbish. But we must make
the best of things. It could be worse, you could be
in a wheelchair.' 'But I am!' 'No you're not – there's
no wheelchair access to the confessional.' 'Just kidding
Father.' 'Three Hail Marys for pretending you were
disabled.'

FOREVER YOUNG

I suppose old people still look
upon themselves as young, because
they were young for such a long time,
longer than they've been old. I understand
this now. I was young for forty years,
but will probably only be old for ten.
I've been young for most of my life –
it was the norm. But this suddenly
being old really takes some getting used to.

THE BUS CONDUCTOR

Denis Traynor was a friend of the family
and worked on the 92 bus route into town.
He never charged me and my mum and sometimes
let me ring the bell. Then one day he stopped
my father in the street and asked him if he'd
coach him in maths and physics. 'I want to make
something of my life' he said. So my father took
him on, but he still failed the exams and remained
a bus conductor. He charged my mother and me after that
and wouldn't let me ring the bell.

THE SWAP

I saw a fit young jogger today,
and imagined swapping bodies.
I'm sure nearly fifty years
of smoking must have taken its toll,
but to just swap and get a clean slate
again, watch him burst into a coughing fit
and collapse at the side of the road –
what would I do if it was possible?
Light up I suppose.

WRITER'S BLOCK

I told him I hadn't written
a new poem in over a month.
'You look well on it though'
he said.

HEROES

Humans love war,
but if you have
a cause as well,
if your country
has been invaded
and you're a freedom
fighter, then it's a very
exhilarating experience.
To be in the right and have
an excuse to kill – what can
be more satisfying – every young
man's dream – the chance to become
a hero.

CREAKING GATE

He's an alcoholic with only one lung,
but a creaking gate never breaks he sez.
He has heart-failure and COPD, but a creaking gate
never breaks he sez.
He has diabetes, gout and sleep apnea,
but a creaking gate never breaks he sez.
He has asthma, diverticulitis and high blood pressure,
but a creaking gate never breaks he sez.
But you have an appalling quality of life I said.
Who needs quality, a creaking gate never breaks he said.

THE NEST

Cutting back some tree branches
on the allotment, I accidentally
exposed a bird's nest concealed
in the undergrowth and before long
two magpies appeared and were in there.
Later on I heard a lot of rustling and
fluttering about and realized the mother
thrush had returned to find her eggs gone
and I felt sad, sorry for what I had done.

THE BIG MEET-UP

Some people often speculate about heaven
being a really friendly place, with people
meeting up all the time for drinks and chats –
a massive ceilidh. But I wonder? It doesn't
happen much here on earth – lots of people
live on their own and are quite unsociable,
even reclusive. Why then does everyone expect
to meet up in heaven – I don't. I think if the place
exists at all I'll be alone once again, but this time
for eternity.

9/11

The question used to be –
what were you doing on the day
of Kennedy's assassination, November
22nd 1963? Now it's what were you doing
on 9/11? I was walking round the Serpentine
in Hyde Park with my older brother and we stopped
off at a pub afterwards and saw it on television.
My first thoughts were 'disaster movie' but then
I saw News 24. A tall black man standing in front
of us kept laughing. My brother said there will be
war now.

MIRTAZAPINE 30MG

It's used to treat depression,
and is known for giving you
very vivid dreams, I can vouch
for that. They must think having
terrestrial television in your head
at night is the answer – the cure.
But there's never much on.

AND SO TO BED

Some people just give up on life –
go to bed and stay there. Women
more than men it would seem.
A friend's mother did when she
was about fifty. I used to hear her
call out sometimes if I was in his house
and one time I met her in her nightie on
the landing going to the toilet – a bit scary.
She suffered with her nerves my friend said.
But I thought there must be more to it than that.

CAN'T TAKE THIS

None of us are really suited
and prepared for the life experience –
it's precariousness and what it can
unexpectedly throw at you. Some people
though just can't handle it at all –
from an early age are definitely not suited,
and find it all a bit too much, born too sensitive
perhaps – they are the young suicides you often
hear about.

BETWEEN TWO WORLDS

He doesn't understand why I'm
in such a hurry to go and I don't
understand why he clings on to life,
perhaps the answer lies somewhere in-between?

BAD HABIT

I like flicking my fag-ends
into my neighbour's fish pond.
He doesn't know which window
they come from; but he did accuse
the guy downstairs who smokes and
there was a big argument, which nearly
came to blows. This morning I flicked
a cigar butt down there which landed
on his bicycle seat and burnt a hole.
I heard him swearing – not very neighbourly
I know, but he shouldn't put Lib Dem posters
in his window.

DEPRESSING!

Whenever I think of old age
I reach for my cigarettes.

DEATH

Death isn't scary –
it's natural and happens
to everyone. But if it was unnatural
and only happened to some people,
it would be very scary.

PUB TALK

I overheard this guy in the pub
telling his friend how good a
conversationalist he was.
'My conversation is definitely
above average' he said. 'I have
a wide general knowledge and know
exactly what interesting topics to discuss.
I should really be paid as an after-dinner speaker.'
I listened for a while longer, he was talking about
drains in the nineteenth century.

WAITING FOR THE MAIL

I will always remember the first poem
I had accepted by a magazine and how
the envelope felt lighter than when
I'd sent it which got me excited.
Then tearing it open and seeing the words –
We have accepted for publication, I was delighted.
A few weeks later I was round at a friend's flat
who is also a writer and he was telling me he had
high hopes for getting his novel accepted –
'They've had it over six months' he said,
but as I was leaving his mail arrived and there was
a loud thud on the carpet, obviously a large manuscript.
We stared at each other, but didn't say anything.

LIFE

It's very strange really,
who you get landed with – parents,
siblings, friends, lovers. You get
very close, share experiences, form
bonds and then die and never ever see
each other again. What the hell was all
that about?

IN HOSPITAL

What I found most annoying
about being in hospital, is how
everything always seems to happen
at once. You'll be lying there bored
for hours, then suddenly a nurse will appear
and take your temperature, then another will arrive
and take your blood pressure, then the catering staff
turn up with your lunch, at the same time as the doctor
who tells you you only have a week to live. And then
nothing happens again for hours.

MISSING

You often see posters on lampposts
in London for missing persons and
missing cats, but I only ever look
at the ones for missing cats,
as I'm more interested in cats than people –
have more concern for their welfare.
Who cares about a missing person.
They can get lost.

MADNESS IN THE METHOD

He didn't want to take an overdose
or hang himself, and he hated the sight
of blood, so he tried to commit suicide
by running up and down the stairs in the vain
hope it would induce a heart attack. He did this
a hundred times, but was fitter than he thought,
and decided to carry on living, with a slightly
sprained ankle.

OLDER WOMEN

when I was seventeen a very attractive
twenty-four year old woman made a play
for me, but I was a bit uncomfortable
about her being that much older than me,
so I didn't respond. Then in my twenties
I couldn't meet anyone in my age group,
but a number of women in their forties
showed interest – too old I thought.
Then to my frustration when I turned forty,
women in their fifties and even sixties
started coming forward – well over the hill.
Now I'm nearly sixty and it's really all over,
but I wish I had gone out with that twenty-four
year old – it doesn't seem old now.

HOLDING BACK THE TEARS

I would have cried in the street
after my old cat was put to sleep
at the vet, but there was a man
standing at the bus-stop. I would
have liked to have cried though,
as a mark of respect almost and
got it out of my system, it might
have helped, but there was a man
standing at the bus-stop, unusual
that early.

EMERGENCY GP CONSULTATION

'I don't wish to alarm you,
but I think you're having
a heart attack' he said
'Really? I think I'll have
a smoke then.'
'I wouldn't do that.'
'Why not?'
'Because it's bad for you.'
'I may as well if I'm having
a heart attack.'
'Why don't you give up?'
'It's a bit late for that
isn't it?'
'I suppose so, but it's no smoking
in the surgery.'
'Oh come on – a last cigarette surely.'
'Alright then, but don't inhale.'

UNDERPANTS

For some reason my mother was always
showing me my dad's dirty underpants.
She would hold them up laughing, pointing
out the huge brown stains. 'I don't think
he wipes his bottom properly' she would say,
throwing them in the washing-machine.
Once when I was very naughty she rubbed my face
with a pair – most unpleasant. I suppose that's one
of the reasons I lacked respect for him and couldn't
take him seriously – I'd seen his soiled underpants.

TUCKING YOUR SHIRT IN

Odd fellow that Ronald Feelgood,
he was always tucking his shirt
into his trousers and then pulling
it out again slowly. He might do this
ten times during the course of a conversation
and I wondered if it was a nervous condition,
or perhaps he derived some sexual pleasure
from it. I was too embarrassed to ask him.

ECSTASY

Dreams can be so atmospheric and uplifting,
especially when you dream about childhood,
which was all a bit like a dream anyway –
and so it must follow the dreams we had
as a child would have been incredibly atmospheric.
I wish I could remember some of them, probably
more effective than the anti-depressants I take.

CATHOLIC SCHOOL

When my brother was in the sixth form,
he and some friends asked the headmaster
Fr Cheetham if they could organize a school dance.
He agreed on three conditions. Firstly no girls,
secondly they had to wear school uniform and thirdly
dance to the music of the school orchestra. They declined
his ridiculous offer, but he ordered the dance to go ahead
anyway. It was a very embarrassing evening my brother said.

CHEATED

How I hate it when I sometimes
go to bed early in the summer,
when it's still light, wake up
a bit later and it's still light
and I think it's morning and I've
got through another day, as well
as having had a really long good
nights sleep – heartbreaking!

CHRISTMAS DINNER

I can't think of anything more sad
than the Tesco deluxe Christmas dinner
for one. It comes with a festive cracker,
that has a sucker on it which you attach
to the wall and pull. My mate in Liverpool
swears by them. He gets it every year –
eats the meal, pulls the cracker and opens
his one Christmas card from the Samaritans.

ON MY OWN

I recognized the feeling of loneliness
in my twenties when I first came to London,
and it made me quite unhappy. But we are very
adaptable creatures and get used to anything
in time. It doesn't bother me much now,
though saying that I come from a large family
and would have been disappointed and surprised
if someone had told me at eighteen I'd be living
on my own for forty years – how can that be?
I would have said.

ANIMAL

Those people who live their lives
like animals, not thinking, not
questioning anything – accepting all.
I don't know whether to pity or envy them.
Is it better to live that way, more natural?
And do those of us who live like animals
get a better death in the end, not understanding
why – no fear or dread, no contemplation of an
afterlife – could it be?

OLDER

I asked him what he thought
of my new collection of poems,
compared to previous ones.
'You can tell they were written
by an older man' he said.

MORTALITY

Most people don't become aware
of their mortality until the end
of life. But I've been conscious
of it since the age of six, when
I overheard my sister telling my
mother her biology teacher was dying
of cancer. It was never quite the same
after that, and what Philip Larkin called
a small unfocused blur on the edge of vision
has always been there. I wouldn't say it's ruined
my life, but it has taken away something from
the experience and I've never really felt in a state
of peaceful happiness, always slightly gloomy and anxious.

NOT NORMAL

My dad once turned up at
our annual school art exhibition
carrying a toilet seat, just one
of the many things he did to embarrass me –
like watching me with binoculars when I was out
playing with friends. They would point to him laughing.
He would say later that he was bird-watching.
It was hard to fit in and be one of the gang, which I
so desperately wanted, with a dad who was not normal.

OUTSIDE CHANCE

We both had a horse in the same race,
his fell at the first, broke it's leg
and had to be destroyed. Mine collapsed
of a heart attack a little later and died
on the spot. I wonder what odds we would
have got for that happening?

OUTBURST

I think I've rubbed my doctor
up the wrong way. 'I hope you die
in terrible pain screaming for a priest'
he said after taking my blood pressure.

HELP!

I lie on my bed alone in my flat,
bored and fed up. It's like being
a prisoner in a prison of war camp
waiting to be liberated by the Allies.
But that won't happen, because this is
my life and nothing is going to change,
no one to the rescue, there will be no
liberation – this is me until the end.

THE DEAD

'You shouldn't speak ill of the dead'
he said. 'Why not?' I said, 'the dead
are a bunch of cunts, I hate them –
I'm glad they're dead, they deserve
to be dead – I'll say what I like about them.'
'But they can't defend themselves' he said.
'Good! That's even more reason to speak ill
of them – stupid dead fuckers can't defend themselves!'

THE 1950's

Still some rationing,
floggings, hangings and fog.
No dogs, no blacks, no Irish.
Long coats and hats, homosexuality
a criminal offence. What's my Line,
Elvis and teddy boys, Suez, a new monarch,
war in Korea, Ruth Ellis, the Christie murders
and Cliff Richard.

THE QUESTION

I always ask people who are dying
are they scared? Some are and some
aren't and some are on some days and
not on others. And some say they haven't
given it a thought. I think I will be scared
though, of what I'm not really sure. I don't
believe in Hell anymore and non-existence doesn't
bother me, it must just be the final moments of pain,
and anticipation.

ENOUGH OF THIS NONSENSE!

I could have said enough is enough
at ten, if I'd known about suicide.
I could have said it again at twenty,
and I definitely should have said it
at thirty. There's no point at sixty.

PRIESTHOOD

He was always trying to get boys
to join the priesthood and started
on me one day. 'But I want to be
an actor' I said. 'You can be an
acting priest' he said. 'I want to be
a pilot' I said. 'You can be a flying
priest' he said. 'I want to be a drug dealer'
I said. 'You can be a drug dealing priest'
he said. 'I want to be a rapist' I said.
'you can be a sex offending priest' he said.
'I want to murder a priest' I said. 'You can be
a killer priest' he said. 'I want to be a nun'
I said – that shut him up.

SMOKING AT 3AM

I can't smoke while lying down in bed
at night anymore – something to do
with years of heavy smoking and the
damage to the tiny hairs in my lungs.
So I have to get up and smoke out of
the window in the middle of the night,
which usually starts me coughing and
the sound of a cough carries at that
quiet time and I'm worried about waking up
the neighbours, especially as someone shouted –
'Give up smoking you arsehole!' the other night.

SISTER

She's always been very good
to me my older sister, but
she might not have been, if her life
had turned out differently and she hadn't
got ill with schizophrenia in her teens.
She had been very academic, probably would
have gone to a top university – had a successful
career and family, but may not have had the time
or inclination to be such a kind sister to me.

BUSTER WILLIAMS

I regretted bullying Paul Williams
and pushing his face in dog dirt.
Nobody told me his dad was a huge
six-foot-four docker with a shaved head
and tattoos on his face, known to his friends
as Buster. But he put the fear of God into me
when he came charging round to the house and
pulled the front gate off its hinges. My father
looked pretty scared too and refused his offer
to fight him in the street. He had such a loud
threatening voice – he stood there swearing and
put his tongue out to my mother who called him
a very common man. After he left my sister burst
into tears, which sent my father into a rage and
he gave me a good hiding, with a tennis racket
I remember.

ALTERCATION

I didn't know who they were
at first and was a bit shocked
when they began shouting abuse
at this woman on the tube who was
wearing a fur coat, she looked terrified.
The two men shouting were so hostile and
I thought they might assault her, but they
got off at the next stop. I noticed one of
them had an Animal Liberation Front sticker
on his jacket which explained it. I had heard
about their aggressive tactics. I smiled at the woman.
'It's not real fur', she said.

LIMERICK

There was a young man called Will
whose only interest in life was to kill.
He did for his mother
as well as his brother
and was certified mentally ill.

SURVIVOR

I can't believe I've been
through the life experience
and survived in one piece.
How on earth did I manage it,
without such terrible and horrendous
things happening to me? It hasn't been easy,
and I have suffered, but by God I'm so aware
it could have been an awful lot worse.

ENDURANCE

Lockdown again and now
I've got sciatica just
to make matters worse.
The things we endure
in this life. I wouldn't mind
if it was any good, but it's crap
for most people. But we stick at it
because it's all there is, not much
of a reason really – so little return
for all our pain, for all the unpleasantness
of living. You may as well see it through till
the end.

END OF INNOCENCE

I was twenty when John Lennon
was murdered in New York. My father
woke me up at seven in the morning
to tell me. Who would shoot John Lennon
I thought, always my favourite Beatle and
I was confused. I played the Beatles all
afternoon and when I went out in Liverpool
that evening his last record 'Starting Over'
was being played on every jukebox in every pub,
and you could feel a real sense of shared grief.
I had grown up with the Beatles and it felt like
the end of an era.

UNSCIENTIFIC

If I was transported back to the Middle Ages
could I explain the electric light bulb,
the motor car, penicillin, anaesthetics,
air and space travel – the telephone?
I really don't think so, I would be too vague,
and they would laugh and think I was mad.
I don't think I could even explain how the lavatory works.

CYCLE

I'm up at seven
and bored by eleven,
so I go back to bed
and lie there till seven –
have a few drinks, then
back in bed by eleven and
up again at seven, bored
by eleven.

STUPID

Alexander Pushkin, acclaimed
Russian poet, challenged a
military officer and crack shot
to a duel because he was flirting
with his wife, and was killed.
Considered by many to be the greatest
Russian poet and founder of modern
Russian literature, but also a dickhead
it would seem.

POSTAL ORDER

My sister sent me a postal order today,
I had not received one since I was a boy
and it brought back memories of childhood
birthdays. I would often get one from my
Auntie Joyce for ten shillings. There's
something very old-fashioned about them –
they've been around for such a long time.
The Winslow Boy was accused of stealing one
for seven and six I think – great film that,
set in the early 1900's. I always thought
he did steal it and the little twerp deserved
a good slap.

ONE IN FOUR

One in four people have had
a mental health problem at
some stage in their lives.
I seem to know a lot of one
in fours. I myself am a one
in four. Sometimes there might
be four of us out together and
we're all one in fours. I feel
more comfortable with one in fours –
seem to relate to them better.
I'm not sure, but I think my doctor
is a one in four.

THE BOER WAR

I once told a school friend
that the Boer War got its name
from the fact it was a very boring war,
with not much happening and the soldiers
were bored out of their wits. My friend
believed me and then we lost touch. I heard
many years later that he became professor of
modern history at Liverpool University and
wondered how old he was when he realised I'd
made up that story. It's the type of thing
he'd still remember.

THREAT

If you don't behave yourself
I'll sew a large button on
the back of your trousers,
my mother would say – how strange
was that?

GENIUS

I remember telling our science
teacher at the start of term,
that I would probably do very well
in the subject because I was a distant
relative of Sir Isaac Newton, so my father
had told me. But at the end of year exams
I came bottom and everyone laughed. We were
related to him by marriage, not by blood I said.

10 RILLINGTON PLACE

I've been interested in the Christie murders
for a long time and got a bus out to where he
lived in Notting Hill recently. I found the exact
street, although all the original houses had been
knocked down and it was called something else.
I buzzed the intercom of number 10 and a woman
answered. 'Do you realise the serial killer
John Reginald Christie lived here? I said.
'Go away you sad little fuck!' said the woman.

LOCKDOWN

I'm wondering if I've been born
on the wrong planet, I'm so incredibly
bored. None of the wide range of activities
available to us seem to interest me in the slightest,
and I spend most of my time thinking in the dark.
And so it is each day, the hours pass slowly and I
don't feel like reading or watching TV or listening
to music. I could go for a walk, have a wank or make
a stew. Write a letter, talk on the phone, try to enjoy
being alone. There must be others who feel this way too,
totally fed up with nothing to do. Life is for living
they always say, but I can't see the point of it today.

OFF MY HEAD

Once when I was on holiday,
an old chap staying in our hotel
said I was unbalanced. I was only
ten and it really upset me. But my
father said 'Take no notice – they
used to say Rudolf Hess was unbalanced,
and he was the deputy fuhrer.'

CHANGE OF STYLE

When I was young I used to wear
a black leather jacket which made
me feel quite rebellious. But now
at sixty I wear a brown Harris tweed.
There's nothing like a tweed jacket
to slow you down, break your spirit,
remind you of your age.

LIAR

He kept saying his bedroom
was like Clapham Junction
during rush-hour with girls
coming and going all the time.
But his brother told me hadn't
been out with anyone for twenty years,
and his bedroom more resembled a quiet
country lane on a cold winter's morning.

WHEELCHAIR

He met her online,
but she didn't tell him
she was in a wheelchair.
'You're in a bloody wheelchair'
he exclaimed. 'Don't be disablist'
she said. 'I'm not disablist' he said,
'but you're in a bloody wheelchair.'
'I told you I had wheels', she said.
'I thought you meant a car'.
'You're wheelchair phobic' she said,
and you're making too much of the wheelchair.
It's the person in the wheelchair that matters.'
'Fuck the damn chair!' he said. 'Just wheel away
will you or I'll push you in the duck pond.'
So she turned around and wheeled away.

FUNERALS

I remember at my mother's funeral,
my father asking people 'Will you
come to mine, will you come to my funeral?'
And of course we did and my ailing uncle
was there asking people 'Will you come to mine,
will you come to my funeral. And we did and my frail
brother-in-law was asking everyone 'Will you come
to mine, will you come to my funeral?' And likewise
we did and my older brother was asking people –
'Will you come to mine, will you come to my funeral?'
And we did and then it was my turn to ask 'Will you
come to mine, will you come to my funeral?' And I hope
they do.

LOOKING BACK

When I think back, I can hardly
believe some of the things actually
happened. Now just a distant memory,
but once were the moment, the present,
as real as now. If I'd known I'd look back
on those times with such fondness and longing,
I might have enjoyed them even more, especially
with the added knowledge that some things I feared
then and made me slightly unhappy never happened.

I NEVER SEEM TO DIE

Does it actually happen?
Do you die?
It hasn't happened to me
and I've been thinking about it
every day since childhood.
Does it happen to anyone?
or is it all made up?
I never seem to die,
will I ever die?
I'm beginning to doubt it.

OVALTINIES

My sister was once offered
some ecstasy at a party,
but declined, saying it might
interfere with her Ovaltine.

THE FOOL'S SUPPER

He's only five foot four and speaks
with a slight stutter. He wears shorts
with turn-ups in all weathers and collects
beer mats and matchboxes. He doesn't eat much,
and I'm not even sure if he can cook. He seems
to live off oven ready meals, which he has every
night, always at six o'clock. A silly little meal
for a silly little man.

BUBBLE

They were arguing in the street,
and he said to her, 'But you're
the only person in my bubble and
you're saying I can't see you during
the week. You know what you've done
don't you – you've burst my bubble!'

JUST FOR A MOMENT

To have lived a life and been
a human being and known other
human beings with all their strengths
and weaknesses has been an extraordinary
experience and a privilege too.
I write these lines in one of my few
optimistic moods, not normally feeling
inclined to praise myself or the human race.
But today I'm glad to have lived a life,
been a human being and all that being so entails.

PAIN IN THE CHEST

The female doctor at A&E gave me
a clean bill of health, but said
if you get a pain in the centre
of your chest that lasts for more
than ten minutes dial 999 immediately.
She said this several times, until finally
I said to her if you get a pain in your chest
that lasts for more than ten minutes dial 999
immediately. 'I won't get a pain in my chest'
she said. 'You might do' I said.

MINISKIRTS

My dad didn't like miniskirts,
perhaps it was the Catholic in him.
And when my sister got one he told
the priest about it. But when she stood
in front of the television with it on,
he flew into a mad rage. 'I'm trying
to watch a programme on television'
he shouted, 'but all I can see is your bloody
knickers! How would you like it if I stood
in front of the set all night in my underpants?'

CAREER

Someone once asked me
when I was very young,
would I prefer to become
a poet or a policeman.
An odd question I thought,
but the choice was clear –
sooner be a poet than a plod.

HAND-ME-DOWNS

The O'Flynns were a big family –
seven kids and very poor. The dad
was disabled and couldn't work.
People in the neighbourhood used
to give them old clothes and the O'Flynn
children were always being teased by other kids –
saying things like, he's wearing my old shirt,
he's got my jumper on. I remember the daughter
bursting into tears and running away because
someone recognized her colourful dress and Easter
bonnet – traditionally a time for wearing new clothes.
It was perhaps the saddest thing I ever witnessed
in my childhood.

IDENTITY

The gangster Ronnie Kray
and the brutal SA leader
Ernst Rohm were both gay.
If I'd known about them,
instead of the well-publicised
Quentin Crisp and Oscar Wilde,
when I realized I was bisexual
growing up in tough working-class
Liverpool in the seventies, I might not have felt
so suicidal.

NO MORE

I think I will really be pissed off
if any of this outrageous shit continues
after death in any form. I want and end to it.
I want to forget everything that has ever happened
to me, every human being I've ever met, politics,
religion, relationships – the whole lot.
I want total non-existence, non-feeling forever.
The afterlife is a fantasy – a dream for those
who have had an easy ride. But I just want it to stop.

ME

I walk across the room and wonder
who I am. I can feel the weight of
my body, my breathing and heartbeat,
but who am I really? I could be any one
of a thousand people, but I'm me. So what
does it mean to be me? I sit down for a moment
and ponder the question and realise the same
person born in this body will die in this body,
and that is me I suppose, with a few thoughts
thrown in.

TOILETS

He was always getting locked in toilets,
it seemed to happen on a regular basis.
'The lock jammed' he would say. But the lock
was always jamming and I wondered how this
could be. Perhaps he liked getting stuck
in toilets. The last time I saw him he said
he'd been stuck in one overnight in Brighton
station. 'The lock jammed?' I said. 'That's right,
the thing just jammed – there was no light in there
either' he said.

PUBS AND CHURCHES

My dad was always going to different
churches, he would travel miles around
the city to celebrate mass at a specific church.
I suppose I did the same with pubs, I knew most
of them in Liverpool. I remember once someone
asking us both on the street for directions to
somewhere. My dad said what church is it near and
I said what pub is it near.

FEBRUARY 14th

I forgot it was Valentine's day
and went for a curry in a local
Indian restaurant. It was a bit
embarrassing being surrounded by
loving couples, laughing and drinking
as I sat there alone eating my lamb madras –
a fat single old man with a smoker's cough
and holes in his jacket.

FALSE ALARM

How awful it would be to suffer acute
chest pain just before boarding a train
or plane for a long journey. Would you
cancel the whole trip? and it turns out
to be just indigestion, or take a chance
and travel? My late father once thought
he was having a heart attack on a train
to London and pulled the emergency cord,
that turned out to be indigestion. 'Better
to be safe than sorry' he told the irate guard.

SOUND ADVICE

Sometimes when I think of God,
I find myself muttering a series
of expletives and feel very ashamed.
A theologian friend told me when this
happens I should shout Satan fuck-off!
three times and then bless myself.
He seems to know what he's talking about,
so I tried it yesterday at mass, several
people stared at me.

DISTRACTION

I've often wondered why some people
seem to be always busy – don't have
the time to do even the simplest of
things like answering the phone.
They deliberately create these lives
for themselves and I wonder if this desire
to be kept permanently busy and occupied
has something to do with death and extinction.
Does it stop us thinking about it? What we've
always known but can't accept.

CELEBRITY

The singer-songwriter Ed Sheeran
was born in Halifax, as was the
serial killer John Christie.
I have to say I prefer John Christie –
far more interesting, better looking too.

THE AGE MONITOR

I like to know the year people were born,
know roughly how long they've got left to live –
it's a hobby of mine. I was talking to someone
yesterday who mentioned his father. 'He died
at 52 didn't he?' I said. 'How the hell do you
know that?' he said. 'You told me ten years ago.'
'And you remembered?' he said, sounding incredulous.
'Of course I remembered, I'm the age monitor.'

CREATION

And God created Earth
and saw that it was bad –
quite shitty in fact, but
went ahead with it anyway,
and we've suffered ever since.

BEING ALIVE

Someone once told me that I must learn
to accept life on life's terms, but I've
never been able to. I find the whole thing
a frustrating and infuriating drag – there's
always some snag, a catch to everything from
finding a hair in your soup to having cancer.
Maybe those biblical tales about the Garden
of Eden I heard so much of in childhood and
how things should have been made a lasting impression.

PROVOCATION

Many years ago when I was a kid,
my brother bought an Irish flag
and hung it out of the window
on Easter Monday to commemorate
the Rising. Kevin Rowland, a Scottish
Protestant was furious and punched me
in the face. Another neighbour whose
son was serving in Northern Ireland
called at the house to complain.
I couldn't see what all the fuss was about.
My father told my brother to get rid of it,
but I came across it recently when I was clearing
out some boxes in the attic and hung it out of
the window.

ASPIRING POET

He asked me after the reading
what he needed to do to become a poet,
and I said suffer. He seemed a little
surprised and went on his way. But it's true,
I don't think I would have written poetry if
I hadn't felt such pain and despair back then.
And I'm reminded of that well-known saying –
'Happiness writes white,' which means it doesn't
write at all.

ALL'S WELL THAT ENDS

If the quality of one's life
can be summed up in five categories –
excellent, good, average, below average
and awful, then I would say mine has been
below average, bordering on the awful.
I have not really been happy since childhood
and although I've had some good times in my
adult life, I haven't enjoyed most of it –
it's just the way things turned out I suppose,
but all's well that ends.